GREAT YARMOUTH and GORLESTON

THE TWENTIETH CENTURY

1900 – 1999

Colin Tooke

First Published in 2008
by
Colin Tooke
14 Hurrell Road
Caister-on-Sea
Great Yarmouth NR30 5XG

ISBN 978-0-9556013-1-6

Printed in England by Blackwell Print
Charles Street, Great Yarmouth, NR30 3LA.

Contents

Acknowledgements

Many people have freely assisted with information, advice and pictures for this book for which I am most grateful. The illustrations are mainly from my own collection and for some of these it has been impossible to establish the true copyright. Anyone who has a claim to a copyright is asked to contact the publisher in writing. Additional pictures have been provided by Peter and Ray Allard, Clive Manson, John Taylor, Mike Mason and Terry Ashbourne and these are individually credited. John Simmons has corrected my use of the English language and as usual with books I have compiled I owe a big thanks to my wife Jan, who has helped considerably with the selection of pictures, and for her continued encouragement.

The twentieth century saw the town's traditional herring industry slowly decline until it died out completely, the end of an industry that the town had relied on since it was founded on the sandbank one thousand years earlier. In the early years of the twentieth century steam had given way to diesel power and, although there was an increase in efficiency, declining fish stocks in the North Sea and a drop in consumer demand finally saw the end of an industry that had employed thousands of people and survived two World Wars.

Above is the drifter/trawler *Ocean Dawn*, YH77, part of the Bloomfield fleet from 1956 until 1963. When the Bloomfield fleet was sold in 1963 it signalled the end of Great Yarmouth as a herring port.

Introduction

In 1885 William Finch-Crisp published the third and last edition of his *Chronological History of Yarmouth*, a chronology that was continued by A.W.Ecclestone in 1977, bringing the list of events up to 1936. In 1998, John McBride published his book, *A Diary of Great Yarmouth*. None of these publications were illustrated but between them they provide a comprehensive list of the events that have shaped the town over the years and will always form invaluable reference sources.

This book does not attempt to replace or update any of the above publications, neither does it attempt to list everything that happened in the town during the twentieth century; to achieve that would require several volumes. I have tried to select events that have shaped the development of the town through the twentieth century, a one hundred year period that saw great changes in the layout of the town and the construction and destruction of many buildings, roads and houses. Also noticeable are the great changes in the industrial and retail areas of the town. The two decades during which most redevelopment took place were the 1950s, when the town was recovering and rebuilding after the ravages of the Second World War, and the 1970s, when new road schemes and retail developments swept away large parts of the old town.

In 1901 the population of the town, including Gorleston, was 50,638. During the period covered by this book most of the medieval rows, and the nineteenth century slums that went with some of them, were swept away as new areas of housing were developed. The fishing industry disappeared, to be replaced by the oil and gas exploration, which in turn was in decline at the end of the century. Factories closed or moved away from the town reducing the employment opportunities and the holiday industry, after reaching a peak during the 1950s and 1960s, also declined as people's tastes and expectations changed and foreign holidays came within the reach of more people. The Local Government reorganisation of 1974 saw many changes in the way the affairs of the town were conducted and an increase in population as surrounding parishes were taken into the new Borough of Great Yarmouth.

The town had slipped gently into the twentieth century, without much celebration. The first edition of the *Yarmouth Mercury* for 1900 did not mention any New Year events except for a three-line report of a 'soiree' held at Winton's Rooms on Marine Parade. The twenty-first century was greeted with renewed enthusiasm as the town began to revive with new schemes such as the outer harbour and a modernised Marine Parade.

After the Second World War, the large expanse of open land on the South Denes was designated as the new industrial area of the town and efforts were made to attract new industry. The first people to lease a large piece of the new industrial land were the Hartmann Brothers of London and in July 1948 their new factory opened, making egg packaging from waste paper. Hartmann Fibre, as it was known, expanded the factory in 1959 and by 1983 it had become Omni-Pac UK, changing to Tenneco Packaging in 1996.

In the 1950s, any spare land on the South Denes was used during the summer months for caravans and camping, the new, cheap, holiday accommodation of the immediate post-war period. In this photograph, taken in the 1950s, a large variety of camping accommodation, tents, buses, vans, small caravans and what appears to be a traditional gypsy caravan (right corner) can be seen using the spare land around the factory.

1900 – 1909

This first decade of the twentieth century saw the end of the long Victorian era, a period during which time the town had become firmly established as a holiday resort, and the new Edwardian era, during which time many changes and improvements took place. The practice of sending postcards took off during this period: it is claimed that in 1904 postmen delivered 613 million of them, the majority sent from seaside resorts. Cards posted in the morning were delivered in the afternoon, a convenient form of communication in the days before the telephone became widely available. It was a period when the first cars and aeroplanes appeared; London hosted the Olympic Games in 1908 and Britain's first Woolworth's store opened in 1909. The improvements locally included the rebuilding of the Britannia Pier and the provision of pavilions on both the Britannia and Wellington piers. A new public transport system was establishment with the introduction of electric trams and new residential developments appeared in the northern part of the town, in Newtown, where Alderson, Palgrave, Beaconsfield and Salisbury roads continued to develop and land north of Hamilton Road was laid out for a development to be known as the Garden Suburb, or the Avenues.

A railway line was built to connect Beach Station with Lowestoft, a line that required a bridge over Breydon Water, the Breydon Viaduct, and a station at Gorleston. The Motor Car Act of 1903 saw the town allocated the letters 'EX' as a prefix to cars registered in the town. The last two corn mills in the town, Press's mill at Southtown and the Greengrass mill on the North Denes, were demolished, the latter to make way for the Garden Suburb. Two murders made headline news: in 1900 Mary Bennett, who came to the town on holiday under the assumed name of 'Mrs Hood', was found strangled on the beach, a crime for which her husband was later hanged, and in 1909 at Gorleston, a policeman, Constable Charles Algar, on duty dealing with a domestic dispute, was shot.

In 1903 the grand circus of Buffalo Bill set up at Southtown, a circus that included 500 horses and a tent to seat 14,000 people. In 1907 the town hosted a Church Congress, attended by the Archbishop of Canterbury, an event that included an exhibition of over 700 items of ecclesiastical art, opened by Prince Frederick Duleep Singh. The following year, the local churches organised an Imperial Bazaar at the Winter Gardens. The town celebrated the Coronation of Edward VII in 1902 and the centenary of the death of Nelson in 1905.

Onlookers inspecting the ruins of Winton's Rooms on the Marine Parade after the fire that destroyed the building on 5 September 1901. This was the town's first major conflagration of the twentieth century

In 1902 Goode's Hotel was built on the site of Winton's Rooms. For more than thirty years this became the premier dance and social events venue in the town. Today Caesar's Fun Palace occupies the ground floor of the building.

Events 1900 – 1909

1900 - Work began to rebuild the Britannia Pier. The Council bought the Wellington Pier and laid out the South Gardens. Gorleston Pavilion, although not totally completed, opened.

1901 -. Fire destroyed Winton's Rooms and the adjacent Jubilee Exhibition on the Marine Parade in September. The Marine Parade was laid out at Gorleston

1902 - In June a new electric tram service began and the New Britannia Pier opened. A Refuse Destructor was built at the northern end of the town. Men returned to the town from active service in South Africa, with the ending of the Boer War.

1903 – The railway from Yarmouth to Lowestoft opened in July. The Wellington Pier pavilion and the Hippodrome Circus opened. The Short Blue fishing fleet ceased operating at Gorleston.

1904 - The Winter Gardens were erected adjacent to the Wellington Pier and opened in July. Roller skating began here in 1907

1905 –In April the horse trams, which ran from Southtown to Gorleston, were replaced by electric trams. Arnold's new store was built on the corner of Regent Street and King Street, opening the following year.

1906 -The grandstand at the South Denes Racecourse burnt down. The Southtown High Mill was demolished and the first yacht pond in the new Nelson Gardens was built.

1907 - The electric tramway was extended to Caister, opening on 16 May with four new tramcars. The Gorleston Carnegie Library opened in April.

1908 - St. James church was consecrated. The Gem Picture Palace opened. The Royal Norfolk Show was held on the Beaconsfield.

1909 - Fire destroyed the pavilion on the Britannia Pier in December. The first Scenic Railway opened on a site later to become the Pleasure Beach.

The wreck of the three masted schooner *Maggi Williams*, 4 October 1902, after failing to negotiate the harbour entrance in a storm. Many such wrecks occurred on or near the beach in the early years of the century. From this wreck the crew of seven were saved by lifeline.

The opening day of the new tramway depot on Caister Road, 19 June 1902. Two new tramcars await in the shed while curious onlookers peer over the fence watching the official ceremony before the inaugural run.
This is now the depot of First Bus.

There were two large civil engineering projects carried out in the town in this decade. One of these (*above*) was laying the four miles of street tramway in 1902, which included complicated junctions such as this one, where the single line in St Peters Road met the double track on the Marine Parade.

Another major engineering achievement was the Breydon Viaduct, constructed by the M&GN railway company. It took three years to build and opened on 13 July 1903 to carry the new rail line from Yarmouth Beach to Lowestoft over Breydon Water. The bridge had five spans, one of which opened to allow shipping through.

Ansell Place, looking east, in 1903. In 1904 these buildings were demolished and replaced by the second Marine Arcade. The wall of the first Marine Arcade, built in 1902, can be seen on the right of the picture. Today, the arcades form the Leisureland Amusements but the roadway seen here, a public right of way, still exists, running through the centre of the two amusement buildings.

The first Britannia Pier pavilion, seen here under construction on 2 April 1902. The very decorative 2,000 seat pavilion opened on 21 June that year but was destroyed by fire in December 1909.

The Church Congress was held in October1907. The parade from the parish church to the Town Hall on 1 October is seen here passing Boning Bros shop in King Street, now the site of Marks & Spencer. The Archbishop of Canterbury is at the bottom left of the picture, flanked by policemen.

The last working corn mill in the town was demolished in 1907. Known as Greengrass' Mill, it stood on the North Denes, on a plot of land that is today the NW corner of Hamilton Road and Windsor Avenue. The mill, for many years painted white and used as a seamark, was moved to the North Denes in 1851 from a site further south. Thomas Greengrass was the last miller.

BENNETT'S STORES,

111, KING STREET,

(Opposite St. Peter's Road,)

GREAT YARMOUTH.

Family Grocer,

Tea Dealer,

Provision Merchant,

Patent Medicines.

OUR SPECIAL BLEND OF TEA

1/4, 1/6 and 1/8 per lb.

Harris' Wiltshire Bacon & Sausages

DANISH, DEVONSHIRE & OTHER BUTTERS.

EVERYTHING AT STORE PRICES.

NOTE THE ONLY ADDRESS—

111, King Street, Gt. Yarmouth.

Telephone Call Office, No. 114.

This advertisement dates from 1904. The shop, at 111 King Street, later became the Star Supply Stores then the International Stores and was next to the Old White Lion public house at the southern end of King Street. *(£1 in 1904 would be the equivalent of about £88 in 2008).*

Bennett's Grocery shop in King Street – see advertisement on opposite page.

This 'holiday snap' was taken in August 1909. The goat cart is on the forecourt of the Hippodrome. Goat carts were a popular attraction on the Marine Parade where they took children for rides until 1911 from which date no more licences were issued.

The notice in the background is for the new Scenic Railway, which opened on 24 July that year, advertised here as 'Yarmouth's Gayest Spot'.

The Gorleston Pageant was a three-day event held in August 1908. It was one of the many events organised by the Rev. Forbes Phillips while he was Vicar of Gorleston, a position he held from 1893 until 1917.

MAYORS 1900-1909

1900 Charles Somerville Orde
1901 Walter Diver
1902 Walter Diver
1903 Thomas Green
1904 Alfred Charles Mayo
1905 Robert Nudd
1906 Chas. Brown and Edward Worlledge
1907 Frank Arnold
1908 Chas. Alfred Campling
1909 Theophilus Witter Swindell

1910-1919

The First World War, declared on 4 August 1914, was to dominate this second decade of the century. Amundsen had beaten Scott to the South Pole in 1911 and the following year the 'unsinkable' liner, the *Titanic*, sunk on her maiden voyage. Purpose-built cinemas opened, and a new craze was 'going to the flicks'. Charlie Chaplin and Mary Pickford became stars of the silent movies. The war brought shortages of food and women took over men's jobs. Victory Day was 15 November 1918. An influenza epidemic swept the world, killing 20 million people.

In the town a Naval Air Station was established in 1913 on the South Denes, bringing the town into the forefront of the exciting new developments in flying. Also that year the fishing industry reached a peak never to be exceeded, when over 1,000 drifters landed 125,000 tons of herring at the port.

Shells from German battleships brought terror to the town with a bombardment in 1914 and the following year Great Yarmouth was subjected to the first ever air raid on this country, when a Zeppelin airship dropped several bombs, causing damage in St Peters Plain and on the Fishwharf. The bombing resulted in two fatalities, the first people in the country to be killed by an air raid. The town was also the victim of the last Zeppelin raid on the country, in August 1918. The war led to the curtailment of tram services and lighting along the seafront.

Building on the new Garden Suburb Estate, between Hamilton Road and a new Barnard Avenue began, the first houses being built in Royal Avenue. During this period large fires destroyed three acres of timber in Palgrave Brown's wood yard; caused severe damage to Johnson's oilskin factory in Admiralty Road, and the complete destruction of the pavilion on the Britannia Pier, the Cliff Hotel at Gorleston and the Scenic Railway. Fire also severely damaged Arnold's large department store and several adjoining shops in Regent Street. The Suffragette movement held meetings and demonstrations in the town; they were accused of starting the fire on the Britannia Pier.

The centenary of the birth of Sir James Paget was celebrated in the town in 1914. A big social occasion took place in 1917 when Major Egbert Cadbury, a pilot from the air station who, the previous year had shot down Zeppelin L70 described as "the finest rigid airship in existence", married Mary, the daughter of the vicar of Gorleston, the well-known Rev. Forbes Phillips.

The Norwegian barque *Ceres* first went aground on Scroby Sands but was refloated and then came ashore on Yarmouth beach, near Salisbury Road, in November 1910. A few days later the ship broke up in a gale.

Many of the first 'flying machines' at the Air Station were experimental and still under development. They were designed to take off and land on water and were known at first as 'hydro-aeroplanes', later called seaplanes. This one is on Gorleston beach *c.*1913.

Events 1910-1919

1910 - The new Grammar School opened in Salisbury Road (now the High School) and its former home on Trafalgar Road became a High School for Girls. A new pavilion on the Britannia Pier opened.

1911 – The Empire Picture Palace opened in July. St Mary's church became the parish church of Southtown. The last year for goat carts to be licensed to take children for rides along the Marine Parade.

1912 - The Royal Yacht, *Victoria and Albert*, moored off the town and Princess Victoria came ashore to visit Gorleston. The East Anglian School for deaf and partially sighted children opened at Gorleston.

1913 - The first Naval aviator, Lieutenant Courtney, arrived at the new Air Station. Barnard Bridge was built over the M&GN railway. The Art School opened in Trafalgar Road. Gorleston's Coliseum Cinema opened in August.

1914 – Fire again destroyed the Britannia Pier pavilion, and a new pavilion opened three months later. A new Police Station opened in Middlegate. The Regent Theatre opened in December.

1915 – The Central Cinema in the Market Place opened. The first air raid on this country by a German Zeppelin occurred on 19 January, killing two people. The Cliff Hotel at Gorleston was destroyed by fire on Boxing Day.

1916 – King George V made an unofficial visit to the Air Station. For a second time the town was bombarded by German warships.

1917 – Rev. Forbes Phillips, vicar of Gorleston since 1893, died.

1918 - Four people killed in another German bombardment from the sea.

1919- Arnold's store and seven other businesses in Regent Street were destroyed by fire on 3 February. The last horse race meeting took place at the course on the South Denes. Peace celebrations were held on 18 and 19 July. On Friday 18 a dinner, for all the inhabitants of the Borough, was held at eight venues. The Mayor, Alderman Harbord, and the Mayoress visited all the eight dinners during the evening.

Yarmouth's Edwardian Marine Parade, seen here in September 1911.
The building on the left is Goode's Hotel, at that time the town's premier dancing venue and next door is the amusement arcade and Picture Palace of Barron's, the first amusement arcade in the town. The sandwich board man in the left corner is advertising river trips to Somerleyton for 1/- (5p) and on the opposite side of the road is an advert for 'The Vagabonds', a concert party who were appearing at the Wellington Pier for the week beginning 4 September 1911.
Today, the top of the old hotel is still visible above a modern amusement arcade and Barron's has become Yesterday's World.

A First World War recruitment drive on the Plain outside the Feathers Inn at Gorleston in 1914. The banner reads: " Wanted 300 recruits, 5th Norfolk Regiment, Do your duty lads - join us".

This postcard shows the damage the Zeppelin bomb caused in St Peters Plain on 19 January 1915. Two people were killed in this air raid, the first such attack on this country.

BOWERS & BARR, LTD., Electrical Engineers,
25, REGENT STREET, GT. YARMOUTH.

SPECIALITIES. } Country House Installations. Electric Light. Telephones. Electric Bells. Motors. Accumulators for Motor Cars and Boats Charged and Repaired. | *Nat. Tel. No. 150*

CENTRAL STORES — FOR

W. READE,

GLASS. EARTHENWARE.
CHINA. FANCY GOODS.

4, & 6, MARKET ROW, GT. YARMOUTH

A. G. BROWNE,
204, NORTHGATE St.

Grocery and Provisions . .
OF FINEST QUALITY.

WILTSHIRE BACON A Speciality.

BISCUITS IN GREAT VARIETY.

N.B.—Prompt and personal attention given to Orders, both in soliciting and executing.

FUNERALS completely FURNISHED TOWN & COUNTRY

CARPENTER, UNDERTAKER

H. F. BRUNDISH

AND HOUSE DECORATOR

CHOICE stock of PAPER HANGINGS

"BARCOMBE," ALBION ROAD,
— *Gt. Yarmouth.* —

IF YOU REQUIRE TOBACCO, CIGARS, CIGARETTES, or any Smoker's Requisites

THE BEST PLACE IS

R. J. BLYTH'S,
Old Broad Row, Gt. Yarmouth.

Established 1780

H. H. HAYWARD,
REGISTERED BY THE
Worshipful Company of Plumbers, London.

Painter, Plumber, Glazier.
Art Paper Hangings of the Newest Designs.
Pattern Books sent out to Select from.

16 & 17, St. Nicholas' Road, Gt. Yarmouth.

CHARLES WISEMAN,
Builder and Contractor,
40, Wellesley Road,
GREAT YARMOUTH.

STRUCTURAL ALTERATIONS.
SANITARY WORK.
DECORATIONS.
REPAIRS

C. H. DYER,
(Late F. GILL),

For PICTURES & PICTURE FRAMING.
Large Stock of Oil Paintings, Water Colour Drawings, Photogravures, and Coloured Reproductions to be seen

Cheap Framing a Speciality . .

60, GEORGE STREET. (Opposite Aldred's)

This page of adverts is taken from the Parish Magazine of February 1911. Two of the businesses are still trading today, although not from the same addresses, and Brundish, the undertakers, no longer offer a house decoration service.

This German propaganda post card shows the Town Hall on fire after the Zeppelin raid in January 1915. Although this may have been the intended target the only bomb to cause any serious damage fell in St Peters Plain, with another causing slight damage on the Fishwharf.

War memorials were erected in many places to commemorate those who gave their lives. The Yarmouth memorial in St George's Park was unveiled in 1922 but an earlier one in the town was unveiled (*above*) by the Mayor, Alderman Worlledge, at Cobholm on 17 May 1917. This memorial was engraved with 750 names and designed by Arthur Hewitt but, after being moved to a different site, it later disappeared.

In 1913 the *Daily Mail* offered a prize of £5,000 to the designer of the seaplane that could complete a flight around Britain, starting and finishing at Southampton, a distance of 1540 miles, in 72 hours. Eight control points were located around the country, one of which was the Great Yarmouth Air Station. One of the planes taking part, a Sopwith, landed on Gorleston beach in August *(above)*, after the pilot, H.G.Hawker, collapsed with sunstroke and had to retire. Hawker stayed in the town for a few days to recover and then made a second attempt, which also ended in disaster near Dublin, when his feet slipped on the controls and the machine went out of control and crash-landed. He was however presented with £1,000 for a gallant try.

Flying machines were an unusual sight at this time and one on the Gorleston beach caused large crowds to gather. In the background is the Cliff Hotel that was to burn down two years later.

YARMOUTH HIPPODROME

General and Booking Manager - - E. W. NICHOLS.
Almost Opposite the Jetty, Centre Marine Parade.
THE FAMILY RESORT.
Sliding Roof, Coolest Theatre in the Town, Cool on the Hottest Day.
GRAND STUPENDOUS HOLIDAY PROGRAMME.
Full Variety and Pictures at Monday's Matinee.
MONDAY, JUNE 9th, and DURING THE WEEK.
MONDAY, Three Distinct Shows, Matinee 2.30,
EVENING, FIRST HOUSE 6.30, SECOND HOUSE 8.45.
The Remainder of the Week, Matinees each day at 2.30. Pictures only at Matinees, unless wet, then Full Show. 6.30 p.m. to 10.30 p.m.
FULL PICTURE AND VARIETY PROGRAMME.
Variety on at 7 and 9.30. Come in when you like. Full Variety at Matinees when wet. Morning Show, if wet, at 11 a.m.
E. C. JAZON & MONTGOMERY present their latest Revusical Musical Comedy,
HAVE YOU GOT ME?
In 3 GUESSES, written and arranged and produced by E. C. JAZON. Full Chorus of
Frolicsome Girls.
Lottie Stone's Revue Octette of Dancers,
Lovely Girls' Beauty Chorus, Magnificent Dresses, Company of Star Artistes, include: –
TOD RALSTON, BILLY MILLER,
VAL MORGAN, B. S. MONTI, DAN LYONS,
FREDA SPRY, JOYCE LYN, IDA CONROY
and all the Stars of Vaudeville.
Miss LILY CURRIE,
Comedienne and Dancer.
PICTORIAL DISPLAY MON., TUES., WED.,
WALTURDAW'S SUPER, OLGA PETROVA in
TEMPERED STEEL,
PETROVA, the Magnificent.
Pathe Gazette, Chaplin Comedies, etc.
CHANGE OF PICTURES THURSDAY, FRIDAY, SATURDAY.
Sensation. Sensation. Sensation.
WILLIAM FOX'S Great Super-production in 6 parts,
REVELATIONS,
Featuring GLADYS BROCKWELL.
POPULAR PRICES. EARLY DOORS TO ALL PARTS.
Grand Circle (including Tax) 2/-, booked or Early Door 2/4.
Centre Circle 1/6 (including Tax). Early Door 1/9.
Orchestra Stalls 1/- (including Tax), Early Door 1/3.
Upper Circle 9d., Early Door 1/- (including Tax). Promenade 5d. (including Tax).

The Hippodrome was used for variety as well as circus, as this advert from June 1919 shows. Films and live theatre were usually combined in one programme. The stage was at the western side, and the building at that time had a sliding roof, allowing it to be advertised as 'the coolest theatre in the town'.

All that remained of the imposing Cliff Hotel at Gorleston after the devastating fire on Boxing Day 1915. The hotel had been taken over by the military authorities for the duration of the war, hence the soldier on guard, silhouetted against the smoke still rising from the ruins.

MAYORS 1910-1919

1910 Thomas Alfred Rising
1911 Frank Arnold
1912 Reginald G Westmacott
1913 David McCowan
1914 David McCowan
1915 Edward William Worlledge
1916 Edward William Worlledge
1917 Arthur Harbord
1918 Arthur Harbord
1919 William Henry Bayfield

1920 – 1929

This was a decade full of change and invention. Radio became the new entertainment medium in 1922 and later 'talkie' films arrived at the cinema. In 1924, the first Labour government took power and in 1926 Princess Elizabeth was born. Electricity reached many homes and dramatic changes took place in women's fashion. The age of motoring had begun and petrol stations appeared. The 1920s saw the start of a long period of high unemployment in the country and Great Yarmouth was no exception. A Public Relief Fund was opened and many building projects were begun to provide work for the unemployed, such as the development of new housing estates and tourist attractions. The latter included construction of the boating lake and ornamental waterways on the North Drive, the swimming pool on Marine Parade and the continuation of the promenade from the Pleasure Beach to the harbour mouth, including an extension of the sea-wall. The decade saw a soup kitchen set up in the Market Place and several unemployment marches.

Three new schools were opened in the 1920s: North Denes, Swindell and Greenacre. The development of the Garden Suburb at the north end of the town continued and in 1921 the first council houses in the town were ready for occupation, on the north side of Barnard Avenue. The rent was set at 11/- (55p) per week. The site of the old North Battery was levelled and developed for housing, the new roads being named Blake and Collingwood. In 1924 the Council bought the Barracks and 26 acres of land at the south end of the town from the War Office and laid out a housing estate, the first houses ready for occupation the following year. This estate would eventually consist of 382 houses and be known as the Barrack Estate. Allotment land at Maygrove was acquired for housing.

A slump in the fishing industry was caused by the collapse of the Russian markets following the recent war but new markets were found and the industry revived from 1925.

Motorbuses were introduced on some of the tram routes, a sign of things to come, and the Corporation stables in Churchill Road were closed as lorries began to replace most horse-drawn Corporation vehicles. In 1928 a huge fire, which burnt for two days, destroyed Clarke's flour mill and part of the adjacent Jewson's timber yard.

The first carnivals were held in the town, one in 1923 followed by another the next year. These were week long events. Horse racing moved from the South Denes to a new course constructed on the North Denes.

Princess Mary, in her uniform as Honorary President of the Girl Guide Association, among a rather solemn-looking group as she opens Melton Lodge, 29 January 1921. The Princess later inspected the local Girl Guides in the Winter Gardens.

A beach photographer's prop, the motorcycle and side car, was a popular addition to the holiday photograph that every visitor had to take home in the 1920s, the days before personal cameras became readily available.

Events 1920-1929

1920 - The first race meeting at the new course on the North Denes took place on 15 August. The Air Station on the South Denes closed.

1921 - Melton Lodge, a home for children of ex-servicemen, was opened by Princess Mary on 29 January. (This building is now Queen Elizabeth Court). The bandstand was built in the Wellington Gardens.

1922 - Prince Henry unveiled the war memorial in St George's Park on 7 January. The Bathing Pool on Marine Parade opened on 22 July.

1923 - The first Carnival week was held in June. Middleton Road in Gorleston was opened as a by-pass, to relieve traffic congestion in the High Street. A second Model Yacht Pond opened in the Nelson Gardens.

1924 - The town's second Carnival week took place in July. Gorleston Beach Gardens and the bandstand opened. Gorleston Labour Club opened. A new entrance was constructed at the Wellington Pier.

1925 - The first houses were occupied on the Barrack Estate. The new invention, wireless, was demonstrated at the Empire and a 'Wireless Concert' was demonstrated in the Britannia Pier pavilion.

1926 - The Royal Norfolk Show was held on the South Denes. The boating lake on the North Drive and the Central Arcade (now the Victoria Arcade) were opened.

1927 - The Floral Hall ballroom opened on the Britannia Pier, large enough for 2,000 dancers.

1928 - The Haven Bridge, built in 1854, closed and a temporary bridge took its place. The Waterways on the North Drive opened in August. The Central Cinema was renamed the Plaza after being closed for six years.

1929 - The Theatre Royal closed after 151 years. The Electric House opened in Regent Road. The Regent cinema screened the first talking picture to be seen in the town.

Large crowds at the opening day of the Waterways, 2 August 1928. Built as part of an unemployment scheme, the 1,200 yard waterway had provided much needed employment for 84 men for 20 weeks. It was originally called the 'Artificial Rivers and Gardens'.

On 4 February 1928, six Corporation steam vehicles were assembled on the temporary Haven Bridge for a 77-ton load test, before the bridge could open to road traffic. In this picture are two of the steam lorries, with their drivers.

Hall Quay in 1928, before the new road layout, which was constructed in conjunction with the new bridge. The two-storey hut in the centre of the photograph is the bridge contractors' hut.

The United Automobile Service began a regular bus service to Winterton in 1924 from their terminus on Hall Quay. This vehicle is outside the Crown & Anchor public house.

An aerial photograph, taken in 1929. Towards the bottom of the picture is the Theatre Royal, which closed that year, and Town Wall House, which is being demolished to make way for the new Electric House. The large square building is the Wesleyan Chapel, demolished in 1937 and now the site of British Home Stores. In the centre is Arnold's large store on the corner of Regent Street and King Street and, behind that, part of the congested Row area of the town. In the background is the temporary bridge, erected the previous year while the new Haven Bridge was under construction.

JAS. J. DITCHAM

(LATE BURTON),

The Oldest Established Plumber's and Painter's Business in the Town. Quite Up-to-date.

PRACTICAL
Sanitary and Authorized Water Works
PLUMBER,
Sign Writer, Grainer, Painter, Glazier, Paperhanger and General House Decorator,
169, Middlegate St.,
GREAT YARMOUTH.

PURVEYOR TO  His Late Majesty KING EDWARD VII.

E. W. HAYWARD

PURVEYOR OF GENUINE
:: MILK AND CREAM ::

Of the Best Quality, delivered to any part of the Town, and Fresh Twice Daily.

THE MODEL DAIRY
30, King Street, Great Yarmouth
DAIRY FARM: HARDLEY HALL

Norfolk and Choicest Danish Butters
Dairy-Fed Pork. Home-made Sausages and Poultry are a Speciality. Fresh Eggs Daily. Home-cured Hams and Bacon

In the 1920s Middlegate Street and King Street were popular shopping areas in the town, both having a great variety of small shops and businesses.

The Board of Guardians to the Great Yarmouth Workhouse, seen here in 1922. The Workhouse had been built in 1838. In 1930 the Board of Guardians was abolished and the building was run by the Council as an infirmary. In 1948, the new National Health Service took it over, and it became known as Northgate Hospital.

Northgate Street in the 1920s when motor buses were beginning to take over some of the tram routes. Here a tram from Caister approaches the town as a United Services bus heads out of town. The men on the wooden tower are working on the overhead tram wires.

The two pictures on this page are both of the 1923 Carnival, the first to be held in the town. *Top*: a Carnival street party somewhere in the town. *Below*: the town's lifeboat, towed by a steam engine, making its way along the Marine Parade as part of the Carnival procession.

Beaconsfield Road in 1922. Terrace houses and corner shops made up the Newtown area of the town. Charlie Allaway's shop is on the corner of Harley Road, one of the many corner shops that formed the basis of the retail trade at that time. Note the many other corner shops along the road, and the lack of street lamps. On the right, behind the trees, is the retaining wall of the railway embankment, which carried the line from Beach Station to Lowestoft.

MAYORS 1920-1929

1920 William George Knights
1921 Frederick Brett
1922 Ernest James Middleton
1923 Richard Frederick Ferrier
1924 Mary Ethel Leach
1925 Alfred William Yallop
1926 Ernest James Middleton
1927 George Platten
1928 Harry Thomas Greenacre
1929 Arthur Henry Beevor

1930 – 1939

King George V died in 1936, to be succeeded by Edward VIII but before a coronation could take place the heir to the throne abdicated, and George VI became king. Car ownership continued to increase; the Highway Code was introduced in 1931 and 'cat's eyes' and 30mph speed limits appeared. Walt Disney created Mickey Mouse and many other cartoon characters and seaside holidays became popular. This was the decade of the Holiday Camp.

The unemployment situation did not improve during the 1930s, reaching a peak in 1933. This had a profound effect on the holiday and fishing industries, the main sources of income for the town. Work for the unemployed included the construction of a new road, Lawn Avenue, described as a by-pass for Northgate Street, a road to relieve the traffic in the Market Place. In 1930, part of Howard Street became the town's first one-way street and the following year the first set of traffic lights was installed, at the Regent Street/King Street/Regent Road junction. The road layout of Hall Quay changed and a new Haven Bridge was opened.

The end of the trams was in sight in 1930 as more buses took over the routes and, three years later, the Mayor drove the last tram from the Market Place to the depot on Caister Road.

Slum clearance schemes were prepared for several areas of the Rows and as a result the Conge was extended through to the Market Place, many sub-standard properties being demolished in the process. New buildings included the Co-operative House and the Hospital School, in the Market Place, and the Alderman Leach School. More council houses were built north of Barnard Avenue and east of the railway. A new residential development began on Gorleston Cliffs.

Melton Lodge (see 1921) became a Convalescent Home and Crane House on South Quay opened as a Scottish Welfare Centre.

From 1937 preparations were being made for the possibility of another war. Air-raid-precaution and civil defence schemes were put in place; public shelters were built; sand bags and gas masks were stockpiled. On 3 September 1939 war was declared and all holidaymakers left the town and all places of entertainment closed. Naval bases were established in the harbour and the Art School in Trafalgar Road became the Incident Control Centre. The threat of invasion hung over the town and the beaches were mined. Although there had been much hardship during the years of the General Depression in the 20s and 30s, worse was now to come.

Part of the large crowd assembled on Hall Quay on 21 October 1930 to watch the Prince of Wales open the new Haven Bridge. In the afternoon the Royal visitor toured the Fishwharf and inspected the fishing industry.

More royal visitors the following year when the Duke and Duchess of York (later to become King George VI) attended the National Union of Teachers' conference on the Britannia Pier, in April 1931.

Events 1930 – 1939

1930 - The last tram ran in Gorleston. On 21 October the Prince of Wales opened the new Haven Bridge and visited the fishing industry.

1931 – In April the National Union of Teachers' held a conference in the town. In August Lawn Avenue was opened by the Mayor, Councillor Lawn.

1932 - Fire destroyed the Floral Hall Ballroom on the Britannia Pier in August. A new Scenic Railway was erected at the Pleasure Beach. The Acle New Road was re-classified as the A47. Pylons were constructed to carry electricity cables over the river.

1933 - On 15 December the last tram was taken off the road. An Air Pageant was held at Gorleston. The illuminations on Marine Parade were switched on for the first time.

1934 - The Regal Theatre opened 1 January. The third carnival was held in July. The Little Theatre opened in part of the Royal Aquarium.

1935 – The old Star Hotel on Hall Quay was demolished. Smith's Crisps opened a new factory on Caister Road. Celebrations and street parties were held for the King's Silver Jubilee.

1936 – The Prunier Trophy was awarded for the first time in the fishing industry. Arnolds sold their department store to Debenhams.

1937 – In Gorleston, a new hospital on Lowestoft Road opened in April and the 'Super' Holiday Camp on 27 May. An automatic telephone exchange opened on Hall Quay. The Marina open-air theatre, seating 3,000 people, opened on 1 July.

1938 – A new bus station was built in Wellington Road for Eastern Counties buses. In February, Matthes 'Sunshine Bread' factory began production in England's Lane, Gorleston.

1939 - In Gorleston the Palace Cinema opened on 16 January: and the Floral Hall and Swimming Pool complex on 30 July. St. Peter's Roman Catholic Church was built on Lowestoft Road, Gorleston.

Above: In 1933 the drapery business of Winters, 51 South Market Road, was taken over by R.S. Mobbs.
In the 1970s, this shop became the office of the Great Yarmouth School of Motoring. The property is now a private house.

Left: In 1935, the town joined in the celebrations being held across the country to celebrate the Silver Jubilee of King George V. This street party is being held in Row 116, which ran from King Street to Middlegate.

The Gorleston Floral Hall and Lido opened 30 July 1939. Built in the thirties' Art Deco style this popular complex continued until the pool was demolished in 1993. The dance hall was renamed the Ocean Rooms in 1975. Today, gardens and a new bandstand stand on the site of the pool.

Many holiday camps were built in the 1930s. Gorleston 'Super' Holiday Camp, built at a cost of £50,000, was opened in May 1937. The camp closed in 1973 and the houses of Elmhurst Court now stand on the site.

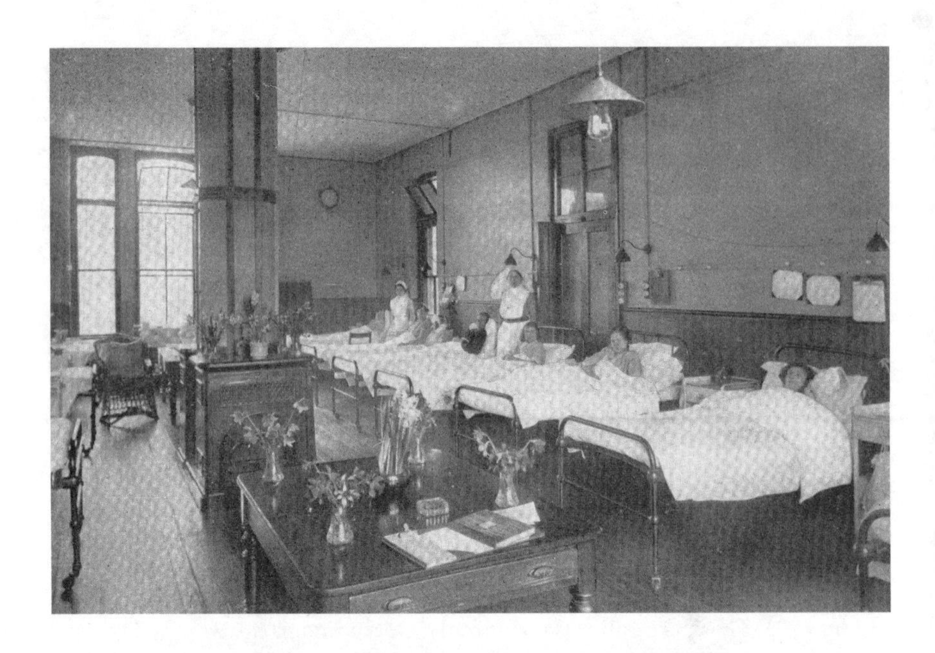

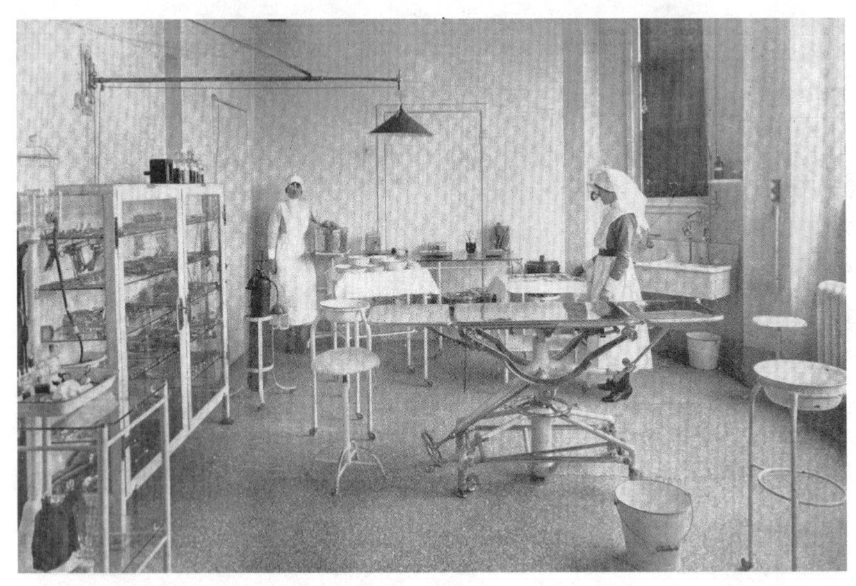

Two views inside the Deneside General Hospital in 1933.
(Top) is the Victoria women's ward and *(below)* is the operating theatre.
The hospital at that time had beds for 72 patients and in the pre-National Health Service days was reliant on subscriptions and fund-raising events.

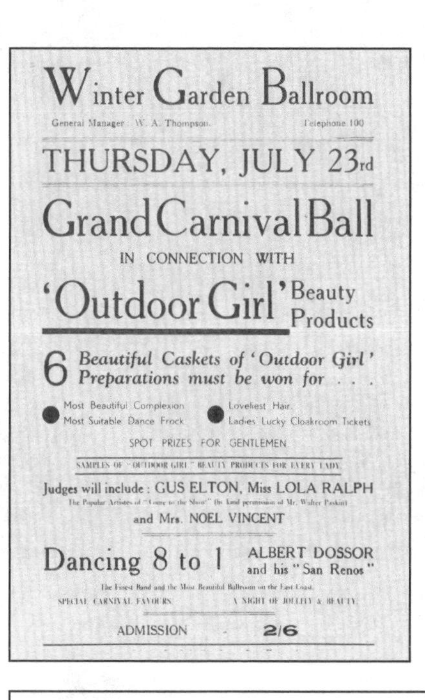

YOU NEED A REST!

COME TO

"PHILOMENA"

BOARD RESIDENCE

BRANDON TERRACE
MARINE PARADE
GT. YARMOUTH

- *WHY IS "PHILOMENA" SO SUCCESSFUL?*
  Our success is due to 30 years of experience, realisation of the fact that it is the "Personal Touch," which makes all the difference, and the recommendations of satisfied guests.
- *WHERE EXACTLY IS "PHILOMENA"?*
  Consult map to see that "Philomena" is in the Finest Central Position of the Marine Parade, has a Southern Aspect, and all Bedrooms overlooking the Sea and Wellington Pier.
- *WHAT ARE THE INCLUSIVE TERMS AT "PHILOMENA"?*

MAY-JUNE	45/-
JULY	50/-
AUGUST	57/6

H. and C. running Water in all Bedrooms. Garages Half-a-minute.

- *HOW AM I TO AVOID DISAPPOINTMENT?*
  Write at once for Tariff and Book well in advance.

Proprietress . . .
MRS. C. TOMLINSON

TRAVEL TO

GREAT YARMOUTH BY RAIL

MONTHLY RETURN TICKETS ISSUED ALL THE YEAR ROUND.
TOURIST TICKETS ISSUED MAY TO OCTOBER.

Restaurant Car Expresses Daily by L.N.E.R. from LONDON (Liverpool Street)

Through Trains from

PETERBOROUGH (each week-day), MANCHESTER, SHEFFIELD, WORKSOP, LINCOLN (Saturdays, commencing 18th June, also on Fridays from 8th July to 9th September), LIVERPOOL and WARRINGTON (Fridays and Saturdays, 2nd July to 10th September), LEEDS and WAKEFIELD (Saturdays 18th June to 10th September).

Through Restaurant Car Express by L M S on Saturdays

COMMENCING JUNE 4th from

MANCHESTER (London Rd.), STOCKPORT, CREWE, MACCLESFIELD, STOKE-ON-TRENT, UTTOXETER and NOTTINGHAM with Connectional Services from LIVERPOOL (Lime Street), and the Principal Towns in Midlands and North.

SIMILAR SERVICES IN REVERSE DIRECTION—COMMENCING JUNE 4th

Also Through Express Services Daily from

GLOUCESTER, CHELTENHAM, BIRMINGHAM, LEICESTER, Etc.

Full Particulars of

L M S Services from any L M S Station or Agency, or from District Passenger Manager, Hunt's Bank, Manchester; New Street Station, Birmingham; Lime Street Station, Liverpool; Leeds, Barrow, Bristol, Chester, Leicester, Northampton or Stoke; and of L.N.E.R. Services at any L.N.E.R. Office or from Passenger Manager, Liverpool Street Station, E.C.2.

IT'S QUICKER BY RAIL

Top left: A 1936 dance at the Winter Gardens.

Top right: One of the many Guest Houses advertising in the 1938 Holiday Guide, the top rate being 57/6 (£2.87) per week. At today's values this would be equivalent to about £146 per week.

Left: In the 1930s, from June to September, the town was served by through trains to many parts of the country by the L.N.E.R. and the L.M.S. railway companies.

Smith's Crisps opened their new factory on Caister Road in March 1935. Previously the firm had produced crisps at a small factory in Cobholm.

The first houses in Hamilton Road were built in 1908, the terrace on the left. This postcard was produced in the 1930s, when car parking was not a problem. The view is looking west, towards Caister Road and the tall chimney is that of the Corporation refuse destructor, standing on the other side of the main road.

The town's third carnival was held in 1934. *Top*: the entry of Leslie & Co., who were motor engineers and wireless dealers at 141 & 143 High Street, Gorleston. *Below*: a decorated horse-drawn dray of Lacon's, seen here outside the brewery on Church Plain.

The store of Woolworth & Co., in Regent Road in 1937. At this time the company sold everything for either 3d (1p) or 6d (2½p). This store, now the site of McDonalds, closed in 1959 when the new Market Place store opened.

MAYORS 1930-1939

1930 Frederick William Lawn
1931 Arthur Henry Beevor
1932 Harry Robert Middleton
1933 Percy Cecil Ellis
1934 Arthur Harbord CBE MP
1935 Ada Mary Perrett
1936 Harry Thomas Greenacre
1937 Eva Keturam Carr
1938 Arthur William Hollis
1939 Ernest Robert Herman

1940 – 1949

The Second World War dominated this period in the town's history. In 1940, Winston Churchill replaced Neville Chamberlain as Prime Minister and every part of daily life took on the mantle of war. Ration books were issued and there was soon a shortage of food, fuel and clothing. For several months the town feared invasion: the beaches were mined, the sea-front sealed off with barricades and roads out of the town heavily defended with pill-boxes and road blocks. It was however from the air that the danger came, the first air raid occurring on 11 July 1940 when a German plane dropped seven bombs on an area in Southtown, killing four people and injuring three. Great Yarmouth was to suffer more air raids than any other coastal town and its designation as a 'defended area' restricted movement in and out of the town. Enforced evacuation halved the population; the holiday industry ground to a halt and the herring fishing was abandoned. Throughout 1941, the air raids averaged nearly one every two days. The most destructive raid of the war was on the night of 7 April 1941, when a prolonged attack destroyed a lot of property in the central area of the town. Four thousand incendiary bombs resulted in sixty-five major fires and 200 smaller ones. Shops, houses, factories and historic buildings were damaged or destroyed. The town was also a major naval base for the duration of the war, many of the fishing boats, and their crews, requisitioned for war service in minesweeping and anti-submarine duties.

In 1943, the Planning Officer produced a report on the reconstruction of the Borough, when the war eventually ended. The report recommended a new river crossing, by a tunnel or Transporter Bridge, opposite Baker Street, Gorleston and a new road, 80 feet wide, from Acle New Road, over Fullers Hill and straight through to the Marine Parade. Many other radical suggestions were made in the report, but its recommendations were never implemented.

The town quickly recovered after the war. The first post-war holiday guide was published in 1947 and in this the Mayor wrote: "We can now offer you nearly all the attractions and entertainment which made the town so popular a holiday resort before the war." By the end of the decade the holiday industry had recovered and the places of entertainment reopened, with the exception of the Hippodrome Circus, which had suffered during its occupation by the Air Force during the war years. The fishing industry also recovered as the boats and crews were released from war service.

Regent Road, 11 a.m. August Monday 1940. In a normal year this would have been the peak of the summer holiday season, but war meant no visitors and all the shopkeepers in Regent Road could do was organise a game of football.

On Gorleston Cliffs, in the shadow of the Links Hotel, a Royal Observer Post was established to monitor enemy aircraft movements. This post is constructed with sandbags but later a more permanent post was built. A gun battery was also set up on the cliffs, to protect the harbour in the event of invasion. *(Ray Allard)*

Events 1940 – 1949

1940 - Coastal gun batteries were built on North Denes, the harbour pier and Gorleston Cliffs. Over three thousand children were evacuated by train on 2 June. The first air raid occurred on 11 July.

1941 - The Revolving Tower was taken down. This was the worst year of the war for air raids: many shops, factories and houses were destroyed in the town centre in April.

1942 – The Angel Hotel in the Market Place became a 'British Restaurant'. Incendiary bombs destroyed the parish church on 25 June. Gorleston North railway station was bombed, never to reopen. The refuse destructor on Caister Road was reduced to a pile of rubble.

1943 – The Southtown maltings were damaged by bombs. Twenty-six ATS girls were killed on 11 May when Whitfield House, North Drive, was destroyed by a direct hit.

1944 – The last air raid of the war was on 1 June. The Home Guard was stood down in December. Gorleston fire station opened. Erie Resistor opened their factory on the South Denes. The old suspension bridge over the river Bure was closed to traffic as unsafe.

1945 – A captured German U-boat was displayed at South Quay. Birds Eye opened their first factory on the South Denes.

1946 - The Gem reopened as the Windmill Theatre on 17 June. The first houses on the Shrublands' pre-fab estate were occupied.

1947 - Ferryside became a Corporation Children's Home. The Police Station moved from Middlegate to South Quay.

1948 - Speedway started at the Caister Road Stadium in April. The Jellicoe Road bridge over the railway was completed.

1949 – The war memorial was unveiled in St George's Park in November. The first Travelling Library, a converted double-decker bus with 4,000 books, went into service.

Queen's Road, 8 April 1941, five Special Constables were killed when a parachute mine was dropped at 5 a.m., damaging Calver's Seagull Garage and the adjacent Marine Store of George Newson.

The end of the Corporation refuse destructor on Tar Works Road. Only the chimney was left standing after this air raid on 4 July 1942. The chimney was quickly demolished as unsafe.

Thousands of residential houses were damaged or destroyed in air raids during the war. This was the scene in Hamilton Road, at the junction with Alexandra Road, on 29 July 1942.

This photograph, taken from Theatre Plain and showing the railings of the underground toilets, was taken in 1941 shortly after the King Street store of Marks & Spencer had been destroyed during the night of 7 April. In 1942, Marks & Spencer set up a temporary store in the Plaza Cinema in the Market Place, where they remained until the store was rebuilt and opened in 1952.

Tel. 2027

POPULAR MEALS at POPULAR PRICES

★

THE CIVIC RESTAURANT

MARKET PLACE
(West Side)
Great Yarmouth

Open 12 noon to 2.15 p.m.
(EXCEPT SUNDAYS)

Parties catered for by arrangement

'Over There'

(Immediately facing this Marina)

BARRON'S

Paradium Pleasure Palace

All the Latest and Best in Automatic Enterprise

RIDES : SHOWS : GAMES
and
PRESENTS TO TAKE AWAY WITH YOU

FREE ! ADMISSION FREE !

Yarmouth & Gorleston Steamboat Co. Ltd.

64, North Quay, Great Yarmouth. Tel. 3439

TWO-HOUR

BROADLAND
AND
SEA CRUISES

By the Black and White Steamers
'Norwich Belle' & 'Oulton Belle'

LEAVING TOWN HALL QUAY DAILY
10.30, 2.45 and 6.30

Fare 4/- Children 2/-

ALL DAY TRIPS to

Oulton Broad and The City of Norwich

Return Fare 8/- Children 4/-

FULLY LICENSED BARS ON BOARD

When you're feeling "Peckish" take a "peck" at the

PIES
from
PECK'S

143, KING STREET, Great Yarmouth, and

175. LONDON ROAD Nth. Lowestoft.

A page from a Marina programme of 1948. The Civic Restaurant in the Market Place was the old Angel Hotel. During the war years this had been the British Restaurant. Peck's well-known pie shop in King Street later became Dayking's bakery.

Left: The programme cover for the first Speedway meeting at the Caister Road Stadium on 20 April 1948.

Four thousand people watched sixteen riders compete for the East Coast Trophy, which was won by Bert Rawlinson.

The team had adopted the name 'Yarmouth Bloaters' and their colours were red and black.

The cinder track was constructed inside the grass greyhound track and was one of the smallest speedway tracks in the country.

The 1948 Yarmouth Bloaters' Speedway Team. *Left to Right*: Reg Morgan, Max Pearce, Dick Wise (Manager), Roy Duke, Paddy Hammond, Bill Carruthers, Sid Hipperson, Billy Bales, Bert and Ted Rawlinson. *Inset:* The first Supporters' Club badge.

The Two Necked Swan in the Market Place, as it was in the 1940s. During this period it was better known as Smedley's after the landlord for many years, Bert Smedley.
Today the public house has been converted into a restaurant.

In 1948, an experimental mail service was started by the Post Office, to airlift mail from the town to Peterborough. The first flight was on 1 June 1948 and here the mayor, Councillor Frank Stone, is seen handing over the mail for the inaugural flight by a BEA helicopter, from a field at West Caister. The experiment was short lived.

Wellington Pier Pavilion
Telephone - 2244

Nightly at 7.30

CATLIN'S PRODUCTIONS LTD.
present—

"SHOWTIME"

A delightful Summer Show with five complete changes of programme.

Featuring **GEORGE BOLTON,** The Popular Comedian, & **BILLY (UKE) SCOTT,** The Radio Music Hall Entertainer.

20 FIRST-CLASS ARTISTES & ORCHESTRA

(Fifth Consecutive Season) Produced by H. MITCHELL-CRAIG.

Matinee Thursday 2.30 Commencing July 7th

Booking Daily: 10 to 1 p.m. & 2.30 to 5 p.m.

For the past four seasons this show has broken all records and early booking is advisable to avoid disappointment.

Admission 4/- 3/- and 2/- (including Tax)
All seats bookable.
All telephone bookings must be paid for by 5 p.m. on day of show.

THE MARINA
CENTRAL PARADE

DAILY at 3 & 7.30

FREDERIC HARGRAVES
presents

RONNIE MILLS
in
'Summertime Serenade'

Mornings at 11
Uncle Ronnie's Children's Talent Competitions

Afternoons and Evenings
Senior Talent Competitions
Special Orchestral and Feature Programmes

FUN and GAMES for YOUNG and OLD

Teas, Lyons' Ices and Light Refreshments

The summer shows reopened as soon as possible after the war.
The first to open was at the Wellington Pier, 'Showtime, a Summer Serenade', in June 1945. The Gem Picture Palace had a large pair of sails fitted to the front and reopened in 1947 as the Windmill, with a show called 'Yarmouth Follies'. The Royal Aquarium staged 'Holiday Merry-Go-Round'.

Above: The Wellington Pier and the Marina shows for 1949.

Left: Despite post-war shortages and rationing, the Gorleston bakery firm of Matthes was able to advertise their catering facilities in 1948.

After the beaches had been cleared of mines the summer season entertainment began to return to normal and, by the end of the 1940s, thousands of holidaymakers were again arriving each year. This Punch & Judy show, always a popular seaside entertainment, is on the beach in 1949.
In the background can be seen the Britannia Pier pavilion and dance hall, both of which were to burn down five years later.

MAYORS 1940 – 1949

1940 Ernest Robert Herman
1941 Frederick Henry Debbage
1942 Frederick Henry Debbage
1943 Frederick William Lawn
1944 Philip Robert Hill
1945 John William Beckett
1946 Herbert Stewart Matthes
1947 Frank Herbert Stone
1948 Frank Herbert Stone
1949 Frederick Kruber

1950 – 1959

Nationally, the Festival of Britain in 1951 and the Coronation in 1953 were the main events of this decade. Locally, the East Coast Floods of 1953 were the main event. Commercial television was launched in 1955 and Premium Bonds the following year. Car ownership doubled and Harold Macmillan told everyone they had "never had it so good". There was a shopping revolution as many shops converted to self-service and the first supermarkets appeared. By 1955, most workers were entitled to two weeks' paid holiday, giving the local holiday industry a welcome boost.

Rebuilding and rehousing were the priorities facing the town as it moved into the1950s. The Magdalen College estate at Gorleston was now home to over 2,000 people and, in the town, work began to clear away the bomb-damaged buildings in the old 'row' area and build new blocks of flats and maisonettes, the first ready for occupation in 1952. New roads, Yarmouth Way, Nottingham Way and St Francis Way, were created and the old Middlegate Street widened, re-aligned and re-named, part becoming Tolhouse Street and another part Greyfriars Way. New shops replaced the ruins left by the war, one of these being Marks & Spencer, who opened their new store in King Street in 1952. In the Market Place a new Woolworth store was built on the site of the old Plaza Cinema in 1958 and the following year the Angel Hotel, which had served the town as the British Restaurant throughout the war, was demolished and replaced by new shops.

The East Coast floods of January 1953 brought disaster to the town, nine people losing their lives and thousands of homes damaged. The town recovered in time for the holiday season and to celebrate the Coronation in June, an event that heralded a new 'Elizabethan age'.

A new power station was built on the South Denes and, as new factories moved in, this soon became the industrial part of the town. The holiday industry continued to recover, the circus re-opened and 'big name' shows, at first featuring stars of radio and later of television, provided top-line entertainment. In 1954, fire once again destroyed the pavilion on the Britannia Pier. Caravan sites developed on the open Denes at either end of the town and by the middle of the decade the holiday trade was experiencing a boom period.

Steam began to give way to diesel on the railways. The Breydon Viaduct closed in 1953 and Beach Station, one of the town's three rail termini, closed in 1959.

Holidaymakers, having just arrived at Southtown station, crossing Hall Quay in the 1950s, long before traffic lights were needed at this busy road junction.

The derelict parish church of St Nicholas in 1952. Only the walls and tower remained after the bomb damage of ten years earlier. Restoration work began in 1957 and the church was reconsecrated in May 1961. The total cost was £342,750.

Events 1950 – 1959

1950 – The first 'big-name' resident summer show, Laughing Thro' with Frankie Howard, opened at the Britannia Pier. The first open-air skating show was held in the Wellington Gardens.

1951 – The Joyland amusement park opened. The *Golden Galleon* commenced river trips. The Hippodrome Circus re-opened.

1952 – The new store for Marks & Spencer opened in King Street. Southtown Station was modernised. A herring reduction factory opened.

1953 – The River Bure suspension bridge was replaced by a temporary bridge. Serious flooding occurred on 31 January. The Seashore Holiday Camp on the North Denes opened. The Breydon Viaduct was closed to rail traffic (demolished in 1962).

1954 – Botton Bros. Amusements took over the Pleasure Beach. Fire destroyed the Britannia Pier pavilion and dance hall. Pixieland opened in the Wellington Pier Gardens. The Victoria Hotel renamed the Carlton Hotel.

1955 – The House of Wax opened in Regent Road. The Guinness Festival Clock was placed on Marine Parade. A new Unitarian church opened.

1956 – The town was twinned with the French town of Rambouillet. A new cold store, the largest in Europe, was built on the South Denes for Birds Eye.

1957 –The Angel Hotel in the Market Place was demolished. Restoration work began on St Nicholas church. The new Tramway Hotel was built in Gorleston. The top three floors of the Garibaldi Hotel were removed.

1958 – The new Power Station on the South Denes was completed. Styles Secondary Modern school on Trafalgar Road opened. A new pavilion opened on the Britannia Pier on 27 June.

1959 – Beach station, the M&GN rail line to the north, and the Beccles to Yarmouth rail line closed. A new store for Woolworth & Co. began trading in the Market Place. St George's church closed as a place of worship.

The 1953 floods resulted in fire crews from many parts of the country being sent to the town to pump out the worst-effected areas. Here, an engine and crew from London are pumping in Isaac's Road, Cobholm.

Boats of all descriptions, including these from the sea front boating lakes, were brought into the town to rescue those stranded on the upper floors of houses in Southtown and Cobholm. These victims of the floods were taken to rest centres at the holiday camps until the houses could be dried out.

Top: Fisher-girls from a curing house on one of Henry Sutton's lorries in 1959. *Below:* A pile of empty swills provides a seat for these off-duty girls as they knit and pose for the camera. In the background is Ocean House, the head office of the fishing company, Bloomfield's.

Lacon's were brewing throughout the 1950s at their Falcon Brewery on Church Plain. They owned many public houses in the town and advertisements such as this appeared in all the summer show programmes

This poster for the George Baines Water Follies, a big attraction at the Marine Parade open-air bathing pool throughout the 1950s, is dated 1954. The twice daily show continued each season until 1963. The show included many speciality acts such as Perry Blake, a diving champion who dived from a 75 feet high tower into 8 feet of water and 'Peanuts' (Ted Cooke) the water clown.

The 1950s were years of plentiful employment. Factories were very labour intensive, as seen here at the Erie Resistor factory on South Denes. Other factories in the town at this time included Birds Eye, Grouts, Smith Crisps and the Johnson clothing factories. *(Clive Manson)*

Sideshows, such as this 'Wild West Show', were a popular feature of every fairground in the 1950s; this one was sited on Church Plain, during the Easter fair.

An oil-fired power station was built on the South Denes and started producing electricity in 1957. Building work had started in April 1954 and 800 men were employed on the construction that used over four million bricks.

In the 1950s, when this picture was taken, the Harbour Mouth café on the South Denes was a popular stop for sightseers, particularly on a Sunday afternoon. The building was demolished in 1977.

The Anson Arms on Southtown Road in the 1950s. This public house closed in 1958 and the licence was transferred to a building on the opposite side of the road. It was named after the Anson family who were large landowners in the area during the 18th and 19th centuries.

Fish being 'cranned out' of a drifter onto a lorry on the Fishwharf in 1958. At this time the herring industry was struggling to survive. The buildings in the background, now used by an offshore supply company, are now all that is left of the original Fishwharf.

Coach cleaners at Beach Station. The station, on the M&GN line, used by generations of holidaymakers from the north, and fisher girls from Scotland, closed in 1959, a victim of pre-Beeching railway closures. Today it is the site of the Coach Station.

MAYORS 1950-1959

1950 Cecil Matthews
1951 Herbert James Shorten
1952 William Alfred Barfield
1953 Frederick James Page
1954 Thomas Cotton
1955 Laura Madeline Gilham
1956 Laura Madeline Gilham
1957 Katherine Mabel Adlington
1958 Herbert Ronald Muskill
1959 Ernest William Applegate

1960 – 1969

The 'Swinging Sixties' was a decade when sport and space dominated the headlines. The World Cup was just one of many sporting triumphs and, in 1961, the Russians sent the first man into space and in 1969 a man landed on the moon. In 1967, BBC2 became the first TV channel to transmit in colour and on the fashion scene the names of Mary Quant, Twiggy and Carnaby Street became well-known. 'Mods' and 'Rockers' brought problems to seaside resorts in 1964 and later the hippy movement reached its peak with the 'Summer of Love' in 1967.

In Great Yarmouth the 60s began with a royal visit when the Duke of Edinburgh visited the Birds Eye factory on the South Denes on 18 November 1960. It was a decade when the traditional 'bucket-and-spade' holiday reached its peak and many big names from the world of entertainment appeared live at the town's five theatres.

A major development on the Marine Parade was the demolition of the Coastguard Station and the construction of the Tower complex, which when it opened included an ice rink. At the Wellington Pier Gardens Pixiland gave way to the Merrivale Model Village and a Maritime Museum opened in the old Sailors Home.

Most of the post-war housing developments had been completed and the largest private housing development was the Peddars Cross estate, near the racecourse. A large number of council houses and flats were built on part of the Beach Station site, the remainder of the land becoming a much-needed Coach Station. New public buildings included the Central Library, Cliff Park School, and the Gallon Pot and Cap and Gown public houses. Work to restore the parish church was completed and the church reconsecrated on 8 May 1961. The South Denes industrial area was still expanding and in 1969 work began on the development of the Harfrey's Industrial Estate.

The first seismic survey vessel arrived at the port, the discovery of gas off the Dutch coast transforming the town's ailing fortunes and enabling it to become an important offshore exploration base. In 1964, the first drilling rig, *Mr Cap*, began drilling in the North Sea and later the drilling ship *Glomar IV* began work, serviced from the port. By the late 1960s, the town had become the largest offshore marine base in Europe, supporting 27 rigs working in the North Sea. A heliport was established on the North Denes Airfield to serve the new industry. Norfolk Line commenced a roll-on roll-off ferry service from the port and as the decade closed the town moved into a new era of prosperity.

The Coastguard Station on the Marine Parade, built in 1858, was demolished in 1964 to make way for the Tower complex, a major development on the Marine Parade.

The Tower building (now the Atlantis) in course of construction. The ground and first floor opened in July 1965 and the Ballroom in December. In February, the following year, the ice skating rink opened. The Royal Standard pub is today the Mint Amusement Arcade.

Events 1960 – 1969

1960 – A new Pleasure Beach entrance was erected in April. The church restoration was completed. Fred Bultitude, the beach sand artist, retired. The restored Tolhouse opened as a museum on 26 June.

1961 – A new police headquarters in Howard Street and the Merrivale Model Village opened. The last steam drifter, the *Wydale,* left port.

1962 – Steamer trips from Hall Quay to Gorleston finished running. The Breydon Viaduct was demolished as was the Coastguard lookout at the end of Gorleston pier.

1963 – Bloomfield's Ocean Fleet of drifters were sold. It was the last season of the Water Follies at the swimming pool. The Beatles appeared at the ABC theatre twice during the summer season. Old Time Music Hall was staged at the Gorleston Pavilion for the first time.

1964 – Vauxhall Caravan Park was laid out. A rebuilt Gorleston Pier was completed. The Sailors Home closed. Tesco opened a store in the Market Place. A US Air Force jet crashed on Darby's Hard.

1965 – The first rig supply boat entered port. Bristow Helicopters started operating. Gorleston gas works was closed.

1966 – The Tower complex was completed on Marine Parade. Down's supermarket (now M & Co) opened in the Market Place. The tug *Richard Lee Barber* left the port to be broken up.

1967 – A Maritime Museum opened in the old Sailors Home. Purdy's Kenya Coffee Bar closed and Palmer's Coffee Room opened. St Peters' church became the Greek Orthodox church of Saint Spyridon.

1968 – Lacon's Brewery on Church Plain closed as did Hunt's soft drinks factory in Howard Street. A crematorium opened at Gorleston.

1969 – The Little Theatre closed in November. Norfolk Line began a ferry service from the Atlas Wharf. Drury house, an Elizabethan house on South Quay, was demolished. Steward & Patteson shut their North Quay depot.

The Airfield Filling Station, Caister Road. In the days before self-service. In the background can be seen two of the Auster aeroplanes of Anglian Air Charter, run by Mr L G (Wilber) Wright. These aircraft were used for pleasure trips over the town.

Another 1960s filling station on Caister Road was the Jubilee Garage, run by Cecil Chapman and Frank Marwood. To the left can be seen the side of the Smith Crisp factory. The garage was demolished in December 1985 and, today, this is the site of the Shell Jubilee filling station.

1964 was the year of the 'Mods and Rockers', when large groups of young people descended on seaside towns, the 'mods' on their scooters and the 'rockers' on their motorbikes. These gatherings caused unrest and the groups were kept moving along the Marine Parade and beach by the police.

A new Police Station opened in Howard Street in 1961 and, in 1968, the new fleet of 'Panda' cars was put on show.

H. FOLKES & SON

DEMOLITION CONTRACTORS

HAULIERS, SAND AND GRAVEL MERCHANTS.
LOADING SHOVELS AND COMPRESSOR HIRE SERVICE

SOUTH DENES GARAGE, SWANSTON ROAD, GREAT YARMOUTH

Telephones: Great Yarmouth **2601** and **62972** Caister **491**

W. J. DAVY & SONS
LIMITED
Established 1871

DECORATING SPECIALISTS

Selby Place
Gt. Yarmouth
Tel. **2331**

Arnold Street
Lowestoft
Tel. **373**

Every Week . . .
Happy Visitors
Choose All their Gifts at

JARROLDS

Great Yarmouth's Premier Gift Shop
Stationers - Booksellers - Gift Goods
King Street, Gt. Yarmouth
And at Norwich - Lowestoft
Cromer - Cambridge

VETTESE'S

REGENT ROAD

FOR FINE FOODS & QUALITY ICE-CREAM

Enjoy a quiet meal at—
VETTESE'S RESTAURANT
Tel. **55631**
in the MARKET ROW (above Hepworths)
Italian Specialities and Choice Italian Wines

D. TUNBRIDGE Ltd.

CHEMIST

41 REGENT ROAD
GREAT YARMOUTH

DEVELOPING - PRINTING
MEDICAL - TOILET REQUISITES

Reserved with the
Compliments of the Directors of

Telecommunication Engineering Ltd.

244a SOUTHTOWN ROAD
GREAT YARMOUTH
Tel.: 4422

For your requirements in Precision Equipment, Press Tools and Instrument Making ——— Contact Us

Adverts from a 1964 Battle of Britain Programme showing several firms that no longer trade in the town.

Rig supply ships at the East Quay in the late 1960s. The new industry was taking over the quayside, much of which had been left derelict since the demise of the fishing industry a few years earlier. *(Peter Allard)*

In 1965 Bristow Helicopters Ltd started operating from the North Denes Airfield. These S55 Whirlwinds, seen here at the heliport in 1968, were fitted with floats in place of wheels. With the rapid growth in oil and gas exploration this was to become the busiest heliport in Europe towards the end of the decade. *(Peter Allard)*

The harbour South Pier was rebuilt between March 1962 and February 1964. Work had only just started when a severe gale in August 1962 destroyed much of the new work, as seen here.

The skipper and crew of the Yarmouth drifter *Ocean Sunlight*, one of the Bloomfield fleet, winners of the Prunier Trophy in 1962.

BEACHOLME
104 WELLESLEY ROAD, GREAT YARMOUTH
BED, BREAKFAST AND EVENING MEAL
If you are looking for homely accommodation situated close to the Britannia Pier, shops and car park—TRY US. We offer a warm welcome with personal service. **Children very welcome.** H. & C. all rooms.
Freedom to come in and out during the day
Proprietors: **Mr. and Mrs. J. BRYANTON** *Phone* 2784

SEA CREST
Mrs. D. CATTEE
40 BEACONSFIELD ROAD
GT. YARMOUTH
BED, BREAKFAST & EVENING DINNER
EXCELLENT CUISINE
TWO MINUTES SEA
OWN KEYS
H. & C. ALL BEDROOMS
SPRING INTERIORS
SEPARATE TABLES
MODERATE TERMS

Mrs. E. E. DE-MOTT
19 BEACONSFIELD ROAD GT. YARMOUTH
BED, BREAKFAST & EVENING DINNER
3 MINUTES FROM SEA. H. & C. ALL BEDROOMS.
SPRING INTERIORS. SEPARATE TABLES.
MODERATE TERMS WELL RECOMMENDED

"DAMAR"
90 Churchill Road Great Yarmouth
Bed & Breakfast or Bed, Breakfast and Evening Meal
(Dinner 1 p.m. Sundays)
Homely accommodation. H. & C., Spring Interiors in all bedrooms. Own keys. 3 minutes sea. Highly recommended. Terms moderate
Proprietress: **Mrs. WATKER**

SEVENA
ALBERT SQUARE GREAT YARMOUTH
Ideally situated near Wellington Pier. Bed, Breakfast and Evening Dinner. Only one flight of stairs. H. & C. and razor points all bedrooms. Children welcome. Details of pleasant holiday flats also supplied on application
Terms moderate Personal supervision
Proprietress: **Mrs. H. RODWAY** *Telephone* 4543 **M.H.G.A.**

"PERIDON"
2 NORTH DENES ROAD GREAT YARMOUTH
Bed, Breakfast and Evening Dinner
Board Residence June and September only
Good food. Spring interior and Hot and Cold water in all bedrooms. Own keys. Ideally situated two minutes sea and Waterways. Highly recommended. Terms on application
Mrs. HOE *Telephone* 55246

Phone **"GLENROY"** *2520*
12 KENT SQUARE, MARINE PARADE, GREAT YARMOUTH
Bed, Breakfast and Evening Dinner
Bed and Breakfast (Early and Late)
Near swimming pool and Marina
● Good food ● Hot and Cold water in bedrooms
● Terms moderate ● Personal attention
Proprietors: **Mr. & Mrs. C. F. HAWKINS**

"BRYDONVILL"
45/46 NELSON ROAD SOUTH GREAT YARMOUTH
Bed, Breakfast and Full Evening Dinner
Situated half-minute sea and Wellington Pier. Excellent food and service. H. & C., Razor points and interior springs in all bedrooms
Lounge with TV
Under Personal Supervision of **Mrs. L. I. BREAM,** M.C.F.A. *Phone* 4833

"ASHFORD HOUSE"
62 NELSON ROAD NORTH, GT. YARMOUTH
Bed and Breakfast. Board Residence
2 minutes Britannia Pier and Town Centre. No petty restrictions. Children accepted. Residential Licence
Mr. and Mrs. D. BETTS *Tel.* 3765

"PALMA HOUSE"
56 NELSON ROAD NORTH, GT. YARMOUTH
Half-minute sea. Large car park near by. H. & C. all bedrooms. Interior spring mattresses. Children welcome. No restrictions. Own keys
BED, BREAKFAST AND EVENING DINNER (5 p.m.)
Terms Moderate
Proprietors: **Mr. and Mrs. C. PALMER** *Phone* 3732

THE RUSSELL PRIVATE HOTEL
26 NELSON ROAD SOUTH, GT. YARMOUTH
BOARD RESIDENCE
Half-minute Wellington Pier. Hot and Cold all rooms. TV lounge. Personal Supervision. Your Satisfaction Our Aim. Licensed Bar
Special Terms for old-age pensioners April, May and September
Proprietors: **Martin and Pearsall**
Phone: Gt. Yarmouth **3788** S.A.E. please **M.H.G.A.**

A Homely Guest House
"SANDHURST"
4 SANDOWN ROAD, NORTH DRIVE, GT. YARMOUTH
BED, BREAKFAST AND EVENING MEAL May to September
Pleasantly situated ½ minute sea front. Good food and beds. Children welcome. H. and C. all rooms. Licensed bar. Every comfort for a happy holiday. O.A.P.s at reduced prices early and late seasons
Mr. and Mrs. OVERILL **M.H.G.A.** *Telephone* 3515

DARYNTH HOUSE
74 and 75 SALISBURY ROAD GREAT YARMOUTH
Telephone 2946
Homely Board Residence or Bed and Breakfast
Two minutes sea front. Public car park near by. H. & C. all bedrooms. Spring interiors. TV lounge. Separate tables. Ground floor and first floor only. Children and O.A.P.s welcome Parties catered for
Board Residence terms from 6½ gns.
Mrs. E. CAMFIELD **M.H.G.A.**

"ELY HOUSE"
13 PAGET ROAD, GREAT YARMOUTH
Homely Residence. Bed and Breakfast or Bed, Breakfast and Evening Cooked Dinner (four-course at 5 p.m.). Hot and Cold all bedrooms. Spring Interior Mattresses. Half-minute Britannia Pier and sea front. Comfortable lounge. Cleanliness and every comfort assured. Highly Recommended. **Terms moderate. Mr. & Mrs. CREED. Tel. 2538**
(Winter *Telephone* Lowestoft 2125)

"BLYTH HOUSE"
79/80 MARINE PARADE
HALF-MINUTE TO BRITANNIA PIER HOT AND COLD RUNNING WATER IN ALL BEDROOMS. HOMELY. INTERIOR SPRING MATTRESSES. COMFORTABLE LOUNGE
Board Residence *S.A.E. please*
Tel. 3329 *Proprietress:* **Mrs. D. E. BAKER** **M.H.G.A.**

"LOMBARD HOUSE"
7 NELSON ROAD NORTH GREAT YARMOUTH
Bed, Breakfast and Evening Dinner
Specialists in good plentiful food. Hot and Cold running water all bedrooms. Spring interiors. TV Lounge. Residential Licensed Bar. 2 minutes Britannia Pier. Separate tables. Personal Supervision.
Very Highly Recommended
Terms from 7 to 9½ gns. *Write for Brochure*
Mrs. F. OLDERSHAW *Tel.* 55650 M.H.G.A.

A page of adverts for guest houses, printed in the 1967 Great Yarmouth Holiday Guide. The 1960s were the peak years for the seaside landladies, and the accommodation offered in this edition of the guide included 473 hotels and guest houses in the town, and 90 in Gorleston. In addition to these were the self-catering flats and houses, hundreds of caravans and two tent sites.

Great Yarmouth Corporation Transport, locally known as the 'blue buses', in the 1960s. Theatre Plain was the main bus stop in the town centre, this Harbour's Mouth service 5 picking up beside the Regal cinema.
In 1963 the Regal was renamed the ABC.

MAYORS 1960 – 1969

1960 William Edward Mobbs
1961 Edgar Barker
1962 John Birchenall
1963 John Phillip Winter
1964 Henry Duncan McGee
1965 Arthur William Ecclestone
1966 Frank Herbert Stone
1967 Kenneth Lionel Collett
1968 Ethel Violet Fleet
1969 John Malley

The 60s in colour

This 1960s picture of the southern end of the Market Place was taken long before pedestrianisation or a covered part of the market had been considered.

The Haven Bridge open to let a coaster through. In the 60s coasters travelled upriver as far as Norwich. In the foreground is the pleasure steamer *Southtown*, which sailed from Hall Quay to Gorleston during the summer months.

The North Quay Yacht Station. In the background the road joining North Quay to Lawn Avenue passes the river side of the White Swan. On the extreme right the white building forms part of Laughing Image Corner.

The *Golden Galleon* was built in 1940 as an Admiralty Fairmile B Motor Launch, ML162. She began a career as a pleasure boat in 1951 and is seen here on a 2-hour cruise to Reedham in the 1960s. The boat, which could take 247 passengers, was eventually broken up at St Olaves in 2006.

The Marine Parade and the open-air Swimming Pool *c.*1960. This pool was demolished in 1979 to make way for the Marina Centre.

The sea-water pool, with diving boards at the southern end, was 100 yards (91.5m) long and 25 yards (23m) wide. It was used for swimming galas, competition swimming and, during the summer months, the popular 'Water Follies Show'.

Regent Road, looking towards the sea. The buildings on the left were demolished to make way for the Market Relief Road, which joined Fullers Hill with Alexander Road (on the right).

The traffic island at the top of Regent Road has gone and the Royal Aquarium, seen here in 1962 when the summer show starred Anne Shelton, Don Arrol and the King Brothers in '*TV Tops*' is now the Hollywood cinema.

In May 1967 the old Sailors Home on the Marine Parade reopened as the Maritime Museum for East Anglia. Many of the exhibits from this museum are now on display in the Time and Tide Museum.

In 1964 the Windmill Theatre staged Olde Tyme Music Hall, a summer show that ran for twenty weeks. The 'Stagecoach' was a popular children's ride in the gardens south of the Jetty.

In the 1960s the Waterways were a popular tourist attraction. The five original boats had large decorative heads affixed to the bows. Made by the corporation carpenters' these depicted a fish (shown here), an elephant, bird, horse and cow.

In 1966 the Wellington Pier Winter Garden was transformed into the Biergarten, an Austrian themed venue. On the opening night the pianist Mrs Mills was the guest artist, the regular entertainer being Josef Hofer and his Tyrolean Band.

Gorleston Lower Parade has changed little since the 1960s. The Floral Hall has become the Ocean Rooms, the pony rides have gone and the swimming pool has been replaced by a garden and new bandstand.

The dining room at Gorleston Super Holiday Camp in 1962. The average holiday camp at that time was usually considered rather basic, but at Gorleston the tablecloths and neatly dressed waiters add an air of class.

The Nelson Garden's boating lakes, before they became an extension of the nearby Pleasure Beach. Boating lakes at either end of the sea front were a popular amenity with the younger holidaymakers in the 1960s.

The brick built power station and the caravans in this 1960s scene have gone and this part of the South Beach has disappeared for ever under the new Outer Harbour complex.

1970 – 1979

Decimalisation was introduced in 1971. A three-day week was introduced in 1972 to save electricity during the miners' strike. This was followed by a series of other strikes that culminated in the 'winter of discontent' in 1979. The 'punk' and 'skinhead' cultures emerged, hot pants became fashionable and teeny boppers became the latest group to enter the pop music scene. The Vietnam War was taking place and many TV shows and films portrayed this. *Star Wars* became a big hit with cinemagoers, as did John Travolta's films, which included *Saturday Night Fever* and *Grease*. The Queen's Silver Jubilee was celebrated nationwide in 1977.

The townscape in Great Yarmouth changed considerably during the 1970s with new road schemes and the demolition of many well-known buildings. A new bridge over the River Bure opened in 1972 and as part of this scheme many buildings in the Runham Vauxhall area, such as Saloon Street and Bridge Street were demolished. Fullers Hill was widened by demolishing buildings on either side of the road and the layout of North Quay changed, Lawn Avenue was now accessed on the eastern side of the White Swan where previously the road ran between the public house and the river. The new road from the bridge, designated the Market Relief Road, swept across Priory Plain, the large Methodist Temple being demolished to make way for it.

Redevelopment took place in the Blackfriars Road area where houses against the town wall were demolished to make an open space and new houses and flats built on the opposite side of the road, the area which had been Boreham, Clarence, Louise and Abyssinia Roads. Work to clear a site for the Market Gates Shopping Centre and car park led to the demolition of Jubilee Place and Fish Street, in Theatre Plain the large building known as the Conservative Club, and the Electric House in Regent Road. Havenbridge house was built on the site of the Steward & Patteson offices and stores and in 1976 the remaining part of Laughing Image Corner and Rainbow Square on North Quay were demolished to make way for a new Post Office sorting office. On Marine Parade the Marina open-air theatre and adjacent swimming pool were demolished.

Gorleston did not escape the redevelopments: in the High Street a new shopping precinct was built and the Coliseum Cinema was demolished and replaced by shops. The site of the Gorleston Holiday Camp became the residential development of Elmhurst Court and the gas holders, part of the Gorleston Gas Works on Southtown Road, were removed.

The fishing industry had become a memory and the oil and gas industry was booming, the first oil from the North Sea being pumped ashore in 1975. The port was busy with rig supply boats.

It was a decade when the administration of the town changed with the implementation of the Local Government Act of 1974. This Act created the Great Yarmouth Borough District Council, over twenty parishes from Hopton to Winterton being brought into the new administration giving the Borough a population of over 70,000 people. The new council had forty-eight members and a new charter gave the newly-formed district the status of a Borough, enabling the ancient office of Mayor to be retained, the first mayor of the Borough District Council being Jack Bishop. Many services previously run by the local council, such as education, police, libraries, roads and social services were now taken over, and run by, the Norfolk County Council.

In 1970 a team from the town appeared on TV's 'It's a Knockout' and were seen by an estimated 200 million people when they played in the finals in Berlin. For the duration of the national fire fighters' strike in 1977, men from the 1st Battalion the Worcestershire & Sherwood Foresters Regiment provide fire cover in the town with their 'Green Goddess' fire engines. These military firemen were stationed at the York Road Drill Hall for three months.

The 1970s was definitely the decade of demolition, rebuilding and reorganisation.

For the last few seasons before the Marina open-air theatre closed in 1979 it was converted into 'Cowtown U.S.A.' where Sheriff Danny Arnold presented a Wild West show twice daily.

Events 1970-1979

1970 – Southtown and Gorleston railway stations closed. Princess Margaret visited the town. Gorleston Coliseum cinema shut in January and was demolished in July.

1971 – Gorleston High Street shopping precinct opened in May. Work started on the Market Relief Road with the demolition of buildings on Fuller Hill. The St Louis Convent School on North Drive closed.

1972 – The new Bure Bridge opened. A new fire station opened in Friars Lane in June. The Methodist Temple on Priory Plain was demolished. The Pasta food factory opened.

1973 – Havenbridge House on North Quay opened. The Dutch coaster *Polaris* beached near the harbour mouth. Gorleston Holiday Camp closed. Lacon's Brewery was demolished.

1974 – In Gorleston the new library opened and the Woolworths store closed. In Theatre Plain the Conservative Club was demolished.

1975 – The Floral Hall was renamed the Ocean Rooms. The Market Gates shopping centre, which included a Sainsbury's store and multi-story car park opened.

1976 –. The rail line along North and South Quay to the Fishwharf closed. Gorleston station was demolished. A clock was installed on Gorleston library.

1977 – The new Gorleston fire station opened at Ferryside in January. The Harbour Mouth café was demolished, as was Southtown Station in November. A new Post Office sorting office opened on North Quay.

1978 – Johnson's factory on Pier Plain, Gorleston, closed as did all Matthes shops and bakery. The Tall Ships race to Oslo started from the port.

1979 – The swimming pool and Marina open-air theatre were demolished in February. The ice house, adjacent to the Haven Bridge, was restored. The Duke of Edinburgh visited the town to open a new Pilot Station at Gorleston. The Great Yarmouth Pottery opened in the S.E. Tower.

George Street in August 1971. The following year, Kenneth's Stores, Row 50 and the shops to the right of the picture were to be demolished as Stonecutters Way was constructed from Hall Quay to Howard Street.

May 1972 and the impressive Methodist Temple, Priory Plain, is being demolished to make way for the new 'market relief road'. The Temple was built in 1876 and closed in 1963. The new road was named Temple Road.

Sweeping changes were made in the Runham Vauxhall area in the 1970s. Saloon Street and the Runham Mission *(centre of picture)* were demolished to make the approach for the new bridge over the river Bure, the new 'gateway to the town'. On the right is the 'temporary' Calendar-Hamilton bridge, which had been in position for twenty years.

Bridge Street, Runham Vauxhall, January 1971. Demolition work is in progress before the construction of the approach to the new bridge from Acle New Road. On the right is the entrance to Vauxhall Street and Royal Terrace, all to be demolished in this major road improvement scheme.

The Electric House, on the right of this 1971 photograph, was demolished in 1974, the site to become part of the Market Gates Shopping Centre. Diver's public house, in the background, closed in 1974 and was demolished in 1979.

Fish Street, leading from South Market Road to Theatre Plain, disappeared in 1973 with the Market Gates development. On the left of the street, in this 1971 photograph, is the Gospel Hall or Brethren Assembly Hall.

The Mississippi Paddle Boat and the Whirl-A-Boats, constructed by Botton's in 1970, on the Nelson Gardens Yacht Ponds. In the background is the fountain in the north pond. In 1972, the Water Chute replaced the boats in the south pond.

Popular attractions for children throughout the 1970s were the pony rides and the stagecoach and lifeboat rides in the gardens south of the Jetty, now the site of Amazonia and the Sea Life Centre. Also seen here are the domed kiosks either side of the entrance to the Jetty. In the background are three pubs, the Marine, the Barking Smack and the Bath Hotel.

Top left: Pleasure flights from the North Denes Airfield in 1975.
Top right and above: two advertisements from the Yarmouth Mercury of 1970 when a guinea (£1.5p) was still common on price tickets in many shops.
Norfolk Radio became Hughes TV in 1976.
Household appliances were relatively expensive in the 1970s, £70 in 1970 would be the equivalent of £780 in 2008.

Work to construct the new bridge over the Bure also included a realignment of the road on North Quay. Instead of the road passing on the river side of the White Swan it was altered to pass on the east side. Here the road works are in progress in August 1971, the White Swan is on the left and on the right the Rampart Road Maltings, demolished in 1972 and a new Telephone Exchange later built on the site.

The south east corner of Fullers Hill being demolished in January 1971. The new Market Relief Road would soon pass through this site with the Falcon Court residential development built to the south.

Animal acts were still to be seen at the Hippodrome Circus in the 1970s. Here Mary Chipperfield's African Elephant performs in June 1971.

MAYORS 1970-1979

1970 Kenneth Henry Hammerton
1971 Alfred William Harvey
1972 Cora Batley
1973 William John Davy
1974 John Milton Bishop
1975 Ernest James Craske
1976 Joseph Alexander Laird
1977 Henry Samuel Miller
1978 George Trevor Scott
1979 John Phillip Clymer

1980 –1989

Politically the 1980s were dominated by Margaret Thatcher's Conservative government, a period which saw many state-owned industries privatised. There were wars in the Falklands and the Middle East and, as communism collapsed, the 40-year-old Iron Curtain was swept away. Channel 4 television began transmission and there were two royal weddings, Prince Charles and Diana Spencer in 1981 and Prince Andrew and Sarah Ferguson in 1986.

In the 1980s, the town became established as the largest supply and off-shore base serving the gas production in the southern sector of the North Sea. There were 140 firms in the town directly related to the offshore industry. A roll-on roll-off ferry was operating a three times a day service to the Dutch port of Scheveningen.

Compared to the previous decade, there was not much new development or redevelopment in the town. Tesco opened a new store on the site of Lacon's brewery in 1980 and the following year the Marina Leisure Centre, complete with indoor swimming pool, opened on the Marine Parade. Debenham's large department store in King Street closed and the building was converted into smaller retail units. Sainsbury's moved from the Market Gates to a new store on the site of Grouts Silk Factory on St Nicholas Road and Asda opened a store in Runham Vauxhall. The new Breydon Bridge and the Western By-pass opened to divert traffic from the town centre and the Market Place and part of Regent Road were pedestrianised.

Industry in the town was in decline. Birds Eye moved all their production to Lowestoft in 1986; the factory of Smiths Crisps on Caister Road closed and was demolished; and Erie Resistor was divided into smaller companies. The power station closed, as did the large timber yards of Palgrave Brown on Southtown Road.

Cinema One became the Royalty in 1984, the ABC cinema became the Cannon for a short while before it was closed and demolished, and the Regent changed into a bingo hall. The new James Paget hospital at Gorleston opened and the old hospital on Deneside was demolished. New telephone exchanges were opened at Gorleston and on North Quay.

In 1985, Her Majesty the Queen, accompanied by the Duke of Edinburgh, made an official visit to the town, the first visit by a reigning monarch for sixty-nine years. In 1988 a beacon (part of a country-wide chain of beacons) was erected in the Anchor Gardens on Marine Parade as part of the Fire Over England celebrations to mark the 400th anniversary of the Armada.

Two wrecks which occurred on the beach in the 1980s.
Top: the wreck of the *Luna*, a brigantine driven ashore between Yarmouth and Caister on 11 October 1980. The boat was quickly broken up by the seas, leaving a sight reminiscent of the 19th century, with scavengers taking away anything useful. *Below*: The coaster *Stern*, stranded for a short time on the beach south of the Wellington Pier in March 1986.

Events 1980 – 1989

1980 – A new Tesco store on Church Plain was opened by Russ Abbott in July. The Yarmouth Mercury celebrated its centenary.

1981 – The Marina Leisure Centre opened in May. The first patients were transferred to the new James Paget Hospital. The Tall Ships race started from the port in July.

1982 –The Regent closed as a cinema. At Gorleston the East Norfolk 6th Form College opened on the Alderman Leach School site.

1983 – In January Smiths Crisp factory closed.. A cannon, dug up on Southtown Road outside the Armoury, was placed outside the Fishermen's Hospital. Jewson's timber yards were demolished.

1984 – The Regent reopened as a bingo hall in June. Demolition of the old hospital on Deneside began in July. The new telephone exchange on North Quay was brought into service in August.

1985 – Debenham's, formerly Arnolds, closed in June. McDonalds opened their first fast food outlet in the town in November. The East Anglian School at Gorleston, for deaf and partially-sighted children, closed. Her Majesty the Queen visited the town on 1 August.

1986 – The Breydon Bridge and the Western by-pass opened in March. Birds Eye closed their South Denes factory in June. The Bure Hotel on Caister Road was demolished.

1987 – The ABC cinema was renamed the Cannon. New Marine Parade illuminations were switched on. The Central Arcade was renamed the Victoria Arcade after a modernisation scheme.

1988 – The Market Place was pedestrianised in August. The Tower Curing Works (now the Time & Tide Museum) closed. The Cannon cinema closed.

1989 – Asda opened on the site of the railway goods yard and Sainsbury's moved from Market Gates to a new store in St Nicholas Road. The Sea Life Centre opened. The Flying Banana buses began operating. Part of Regent Road was pedestrianised.

The Bath Hotel in March 1987 when the ground floor was the Circus Tavern. Today this is the Flamingo Amusement Arcade.

The old lifeboat house on Marine Parade has been used for many things over the years; in the 1980s it was Terror Castle, becoming Ghost Busters in 1990. The building is today the Mission bar and night club.

A popular children's amusement for over thirty years, these pedal cars on Marine Parade were removed in 1989 to make way for the Sea Life Centre to be built on the site.

This engine shed, and other railway buildings, on the site of the Vauxhall Goods Yard were demolished in the 1980s and an Asda supermarket built on the site, opening on 24 May 1989. The buildings that were demolished were the last examples of nineteenth railway architecture left in the town.

BROADS CRUISES

BOOKING AND SAILING FROM HALL QUAY
Telephone: 3642, 3661 & 62510

'THE BROADLAND BELLE'

A Continental styled water bus

TUESDAY, WEDNESDAY and THURSDAY

OULTON BROAD

A LONG DISTANCE CRUISE
APPROX. 2 HOURS ASHORE MID-DAY

Via Rivers Yare and Waveney, Burgh Castle, Belton, Somerleyton and Oulton Dyke

DEPART 10.00 **(REDUCED FARES FOR CHILDREN)** RETURN 5.15 APPROX

SUNDAY, MONDAY and FRIDAY
Departures 10.30, 2.45 Returning 12.30, 4.45
Every evening, light permitting, except Saturday, 6.30 to 8.30

BROADLAND CRUISES

NON-STOP VIA BREYDON WATER & BERNEY ARMS WINDMILL

(REDUCED FARES FOR CHILDREN)

SKATE SHOW 82

MONDAYS & THURSDAYS AT 7.30 pm
ADMISSION 75p, ALL CLASSES, BUT PARTIES OF TWENTY AND OVER 60p.
A SUPER FAMILY SHOW FEATURING
GRAHAM CUBITT,
VALERIE STOTT, and
THE GREAT YARMOUTH ROLLER SKATING CLUB

PLEASURE FLIGHTS

Over Great Yarmouth, Coast and Broads

From **NORTH DENES AERODROME**

Caister Road, Great Yarmouth, NR30 5TF

Telephone: GREAT YARMOUTH 4426

From 10 a.m. daily Prices on application

A trip to the Broads in the 'Broadland Belle', the roller skating show in the Wellington Pier Gardens and pleasure flights from the Caister Road airfield were all popular attractions for the holidaymakers in the town for the 1982 season.

All the patients have gone and the old General Hospital in Deneside is closed and boarded up in 1984, just before demolition began. The residential development of St George's Court now stands on the site.

In St Peters Plain, at the rear of the Deneside Hospital, was the old St Georges School. The pupils were evacuated in 1940 and the school never reopened. In January 1948 the building opened as an extension to the hospital, housing the out-patients department and later the accident and emergency department. Today this is the site of Ravelin House.

Work to pedestrianise the first part of Regent Road began in March 1989 and was completed before the summer season began.

In the background is the Cannon cinema, which had closed in May the previous year. Demolition of the cinema began in July 1989.

In 1984 the Gas Board moved their showroom from Regent Street to this shop in the Market Place, previously the shop of Timothy White's. David Jacobs, arriving in a horse-drawn landau, performed the opening ceremony. The Gas Board shop closed ten years later and today this is Nationwide Building Society. *(Terry Ashbourne)*

The new Breydon Bridge was completed in July 1985, several months ahead of the road that would form the Western Bypass, which opened to traffic in March 1986.
Here the Dutch barge '*Tak-Lift II'* with the port tug, the *Hector Read,* negotiates the Haven Bridge with the counterbalance for the new bridge on 23 January 1985. *(Peter Allard)*

Flying Banana buses, in their distinctive yellow and green livery, began operating in the town in December 1989. After a few years this independent bus company was taken over by First Bus. *(Peter Allard)*

Her Majesty Queen Elizabeth II, accompanied by the Mayor, Councillor James Benson, starts her walk through the Market Place as part of the royal visit on 1 August 1985. *(Clive Manson)*

MAYORS 1980-1989

1980 Ronald George Webb
1981 Frank Gordon Chapman
1982 David Ernest Arnold
1983 Barry George Coleman
1984 Henry Duncan McGee
1985 James Minion Benson
1986 Brenda Margaret Mills
1987 George Sherratt Johnson
1988 Derek John Maddeys
1989 James Robert Shrimplin

1990 – 1999

This last decade of the twentieth century began with war when Iraq invaded Kuwait in 1990, an invasion that led to further conflict in the Middle East. The National Lottery began in 1994 and the following year the Channel Tunnel opened. New Labour ended eighteen years of Conservative government in 1997 and Hong Kong, a British colony since 1842, was handed back to China. Princess Diana was killed in a car crash on 1 September 1997. In the world of music Girl Power struck in 1996 when the Spice Girls became the most popular girl group ever.

The Great Yarmouth Council abolished the ancient office of Mayor in January 1991 and work started on the £16 million Gorleston by-pass, a scheme that included the demolition of many properties along the line of the new road, which was completed in 1993. New buildings to appear in the town included the Court House on North Quay and the Job Centre on the Conge. St Nicholas Hospital closed in 1993 and was put up for sale and, three years later, the buildings were converted into 62 houses and apartments. Demolition included the International High School on North Drive, the Park Baptist Chapel in Crown Road and the Power Station on South Denes.

In February 1993 a two-metre surge tide caused flooding and damage in the town. Four hundred people were evacuated in Gorleston; the highest tide since the 1953 floods. On 20 May the Queen came ashore at Stonecutters Quay from the Royal Yacht Britannia, where she transferred to a waiting car to take her to an official engagement at Thetford. A disastrous fire on the night of 13 September 1995 destroyed several buildings in Market Row, one of them dating back to the 18th century. This was the worst peacetime blaze in living memory, fought by over 100 firefighters brought in from many parts of Norfolk and Suffolk. Among the businesses destroyed were Courts furniture store, where the fire started, and Greenacre's butchers shop.

In September 1997 an unusual event, 'Out of the Blue', was staged at Gorleston. Described as "more of a performance than a play" the event, with a cast of 500 including 22 ships and boats, 19 vehicles, a helicopter, model boats, rollerskaters, kite fliers and emergency service volunteers, was watched by a large audience from the quayside at Brush Bend and then from a grandstand opposite the Yacht Pond.

Pony rides in the gardens on the south side of the Jetty, now the site of Amazonia, were a bargain at 25p in June 1993. Today a donkey ride on the beach costs £2.

As part of the celebration to mark the official opening of the pedestrianised Market Place on 23 September 1995 a tight-rope walker, George Carlin, made the 300 feet walk from Palmers to the Market Gates on a wire 60 feet above the ground.
No safety net was used and at the time it was thought this was the first tight-rope walk across any market in the country. *(Terry Ashbourne)*

Events 1990 – 1999

1990 – Shops were built on the site of the Cannon cinema. The Market Place was repaved. The Baptist Church in Crown Road and the East Anglian School in Gorleston were demolished.

1991 – The office of Mayor was abolished. (Reinstated in 2000). The Sea Life Centre on Marine Parade opened.

1992 – Norfolk Line ferries left the port to be based in Felixtowe. H.R.H. the Duke of Gloucester opened a new Court House on North Quay on 28 January. Ripley's 'Believe it or Not' exhibition opened at the Windmill.

1993 – The Gorleston by-pass was completed in September. St Nicholas Hospital closed. At Gorleston a new lifeboat station opened and the swimming pool was demolished. The NW Tower opened as a Broads Information Centre. H.M. the Queen made a brief visit on 20 May.

1994 – The electricity pylons carrying cables over the river were taken down. The last maltings in the town, E S Beaven in Cobholm, closed in September. Church Road School, Gorleston, was demolished.

1995 – Pirate's Cove crazy golf opened in July. A major fire in Market Row destroyed several buildings on 13 September. Leach's shop in the Market Place closed. A new Baptist chapel in Crown Road opened in June.

1996 – The College of Art & Design closed in July. Troll Cart public house opened. Empire converted into Bourbon Street night club. The last year of special weeks for the Senior Citizens' Holidays.

1997 – Eastern Counties bus depot in Wellington Road closed. The power station and chimney were demolished on 5 May.

1998 – Yarmouth Stores on South Quay celebrated their centenary. Plattens store in Broad Row closed in July. A 500lb bomb was dredged from the river near the Haven Bridge.

1999 –The Working Men's Club in King Street closed. On 23 December over 1,500 travellers arrived, camping at the south end of the Marine Parade.

The Wellington Road depot and the offices of Eastern Counties buses closed in January 1997 after First Bus had taken over. The buildings were demolished and houses now occupy the site, on the corner with St Peters Road.

The Victoria Gardens public house in Blackfriars Road was demolished in 1998. It was originally part of the Victoria Pleasure Gardens that covered a large area between Blackfriars Road and Havelock Road from 1855 until 1872.

These two pictures show the devastation caused by the fire that broke out in the early hours of 13 September 1995 in Market Row. The fire began in Courts furniture store and quickly spread to adjacent buildings. More than 100 firefighters, some from as far afield as Lowestoft and Mundesley, battled to contain the blaze, which at one time was in danger of spreading and engulfing the whole Row. It was to be several years before rebuilding began. *(Above: Mike Mason). (Left: John Taylor).*

On Bank Holiday Monday, 5 May 1997, the South Denes Power Station was reduced to a pile of rubble, a sight watched by a large crowd on the Gorleston side of the river.

In December 1999 a new gas-powered power station began to take shape on the South Denes, on the same site as the one demolished two years earlier.
(Peter Allard)

The Park Baptist Church in Crown Road was demolished in June 1990 and a new, smaller, church incorporated with the redevelopment of the site. The new church opened in June 1995

The shop of Leach & Son, in the Market Place, closed in December 1995. This family business had been trading in the town for 127 years when it closed.

At the end of 1999, the town looked forward to the start of the twenty-first century and also the third millennium. The planned celebrations on New Years Eve had to be curtailed because of the large influx of 1,500 travellers who had descended on the town just before Christmas, and camped at the southern end of Marine Parade. A firework display was cancelled and clubs along the sea front were unable to hold their celebrations. Many public houses in the town did not open but this did not prevent a large number of people gathering in the Market Place to watch as the Millennium Beacon, part of a nation-wide chain of beacons, was lit at the top of the church tower. As the beacon burst into flame the ships in the river sounded their horns and sirens in the traditional New Year welcome.

The first beacon in this chain of 2,500 across the country, an event organised by Bruno Peak, was lit by Her Majesty the Queen in London, on a barge on the river Thames. The gas-fired beacon, 26 feet high, had been specially built in Great Yarmouth, at the Seatrax yard. After the London ceremony the beacon was brought back to the town and now stands at the entrance to Beacon Park, off Lowestoft Road, Gorleston.

MAYORS 1990-1999

1990 WILLIAM DOUGAL

There were no more mayors in this decade. The Borough Council voted to abolish the position from 1991. The office of mayor was reinstated in the year 2000.

Index

Numbers in **bold** type indicate illustrations.